# A Head Full
# of Stories

First published 2005
Evans Brothers Limited
2A Portman Mansions
Chiltern Street
London W1U 6NR

British Library Cataloguing in Publication Data

Swallow, Su
        A head full of stories. - (Twisters)
        1. Children's stories - Pictorial works
        I. Title
        823.9'14 [J]

ISBN-10: 0237530694
13-digit ISBN (from 1 January 2007) 9780237530730

Printed in China by WKT Company Limited

Series Editor: Nick Turpin
Design: Robert Walster
Production: Jenny Mulvanny
Series Consultant: Gill Matthews

TWISTERS

# A Head Full of Stories

Su Swallow
and Tim Archbold

Evans

"Jack!"

"Story time!"

"No!" shouted Jack.
"My head is full up with
stories."

"You tell
me a story,
then."

10

So Jack told Mum about
Cinderella.

He told Dad a story too.

And Grandma...

and Grandad…

19

and his brother…

and the cat...

and Teddy.

"My head's empty now!"

28

"Tell me a story please!"

Why not try reading another Twisters book?